QUEEN
FOR PIANO DUET

8 GREAT ARRANGEMENTS BY PHILLIP KEVEREN

— PIANO LEVEL —
INTERMEDIATE TO EARLY ADVANCED

Cover photo by Rob Verhorst / Contributor

ISBN 978-1-70511-305-9

Visit Hal Leonard Online at
www.halleonard.com

Visit Phillip at
www.phillipkeveren.com

World headquarters, contact:
Hal Leonard
7777 West Bluemound Road
Milwaukee, WI 53213
Email: info@halleonard.com

In Europe, contact:
Hal Leonard Europe Limited
1 Red Place
London, W1K 6PL
Email: info@halleonardeurope.com

In Australia, contact:
Hal Leonard Australia Pty. Ltd.
4 Lentara Court
Cheltenham, Victoria, 3192 Australia
Email: info@halleonard.com.au

PREFACE

Duet playing at the piano is fun. The music of Queen is a riot. Put the two together and it's a pretty potent combination!

When preparing pop music, it's always a good idea to reference the original recordings. Listen for the overall feel of the song and to glean a deeper understanding of phrasing and articulation nuance.

Happy dueting!

BIOGRAPHY

Phillip Keveren, a multi-talented keyboard artist and composer, writes original works in a variety of genres from piano solo to symphonic orchestra. He gives frequent concerts and workshops for teachers and their students in the United States, Canada, Europe, and Asia. Mr. Keveren holds a B.M. in composition from California State University Northridge and a M.M. in composition from the University of Southern California.

CRAZY LITTLE THING CALLED LOVE

Words and Music by FREDDIE MERCURY
Arranged by Phillip Keveren

ANOTHER ONE BITES THE DUST

Words and Music by JOHN DEACON
Arranged by Phillip Keveren

BOHEMIAN RHAPSODY

Words and Music by FREDDIE MERCURY
Arranged by Phillip Keveren

KILLER QUEEN

Words and Music by FREDDIE MERCURY
Arranged by Phillip Keveren

WE WILL ROCK YOU

Words and Music by BRIAN MAY
Arranged by Phillip Keveren

UNDER PRESSURE

Words and Music by FREDDIE MERCURY,
JOHN DEACON, BRIAN MAY,
ROGER TAYLOR and DAVID BOWIE
Arranged by Phillip Keveren

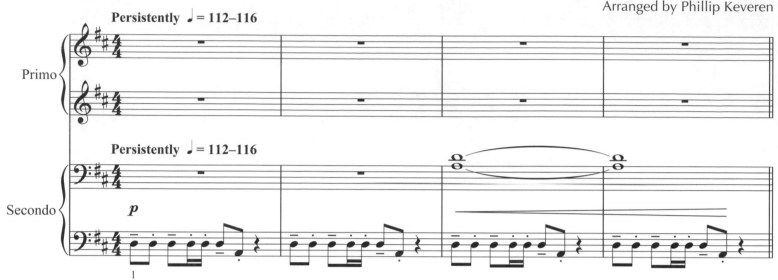

WE ARE THE CHAMPIONS

Words and Music by FREDDIE MERCURY
Arranged by Phillip Keveren

WHO WANTS TO LIVE FOREVER

Words and Music by BRIAN MAY
Arranged by Phillip Keveren

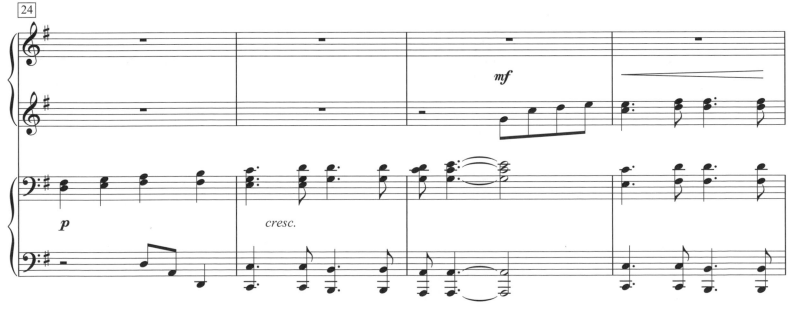

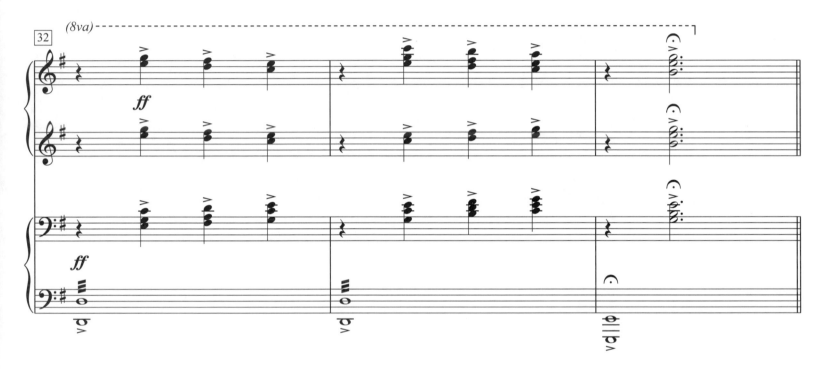

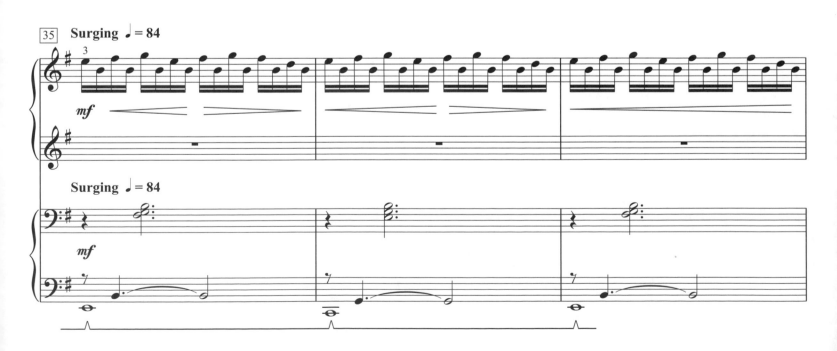

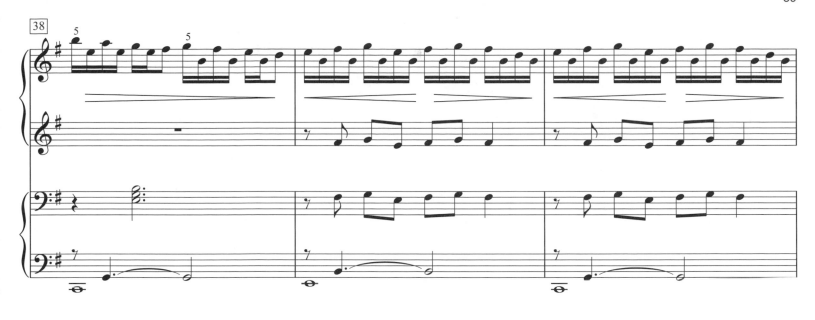